Sikhism

Davinder Kaur Babraa

Series editor: Clive Erricker

Longman

About the *Religions through Festivals* series

Festivals are ways of remembering who we are and where we belong. Religious festivals are ways in which people of one faith celebrate their belonging together.

These are not only times of great joy but also of serious reflection – two aspects of festivals which, when brought together, provide a clear way for people to understand the meaning of a faith for a believer and for a community.

This series looks at six great religious traditions – Hinduism, Buddhism, Islam, Christianity, Judaism and Sikhism – through their festivals. One thing that will become clear, when you read these books, is just how different each of the faiths is. With this in mind, each author has approached his or her task in the way best suited to convey a feeling for the specialness of each religion.

All six books are concerned, not only with conveying information, but also with ways of learning, because real understanding results from the way we learn as well as what we learn.

Each spread in each book offers plenty of variety for learning to take place, in the use of pictures and activities as well as text so that the skill of learning about a religious faith will grow progressively as you use and enjoy the books.

About *Sikhism*

Although Sikhism is a fairly new religion, it is one of the major religions of the world. Sikhism began in the Punjab, a north-western region of India. Today Sikhs are found in most parts of the world. About 300,000 of the 14 million Sikhs of the world live in Britain. Whilst there are many subtle cultural differences amongst Sikhs, depending on where they live, there is no religious difference because all Sikhs follow the teachings of their ten Gurus and the book of scriptures. From 1469 to 1708, Sikhs not only acquired their own scriptures, but also developed their own distinctive marriage and initiation practices. The appearance of adult male Sikhs, characterised by their beards and colourful turbans, often intrigues people who know little or nothing about Sikhs. This book tries to tell you more about Sikhs and their religion through their festivals.

Contents

1   Where is your home?

Home is a very special place. More than anywhere else it is where you belong. For some groups of people there is a particular place in the world they think of as their *homeland*, a place where they belong even if some of them now live somewhere else. For Sikh people their homeland is a place called the **Punjab** in India. Many Sikhs still live there; however, we shall read about a Sikh family who now live in Britain and return to the Punjab only for a special holiday.

The Land of the Five Rivers

When India became independent in 1947 the Punjab was divided into two parts. Today, it is much smaller than before. This is because once again in 1966 it was divided by the Indian Government – creating two more states: Haryana and Himachal Pradesh.

The Punjab is the centre of Sikh culture and tradition. Most of the Sikh shrines are in the Punjab. Though many Sikhs have moved from villages to towns and cities to set up different industries and business, farming remains the main occupation of Sikhs. Using modern farming methods and modern equipment they have greatly improved the Punjab agriculture. In fact, the Punjab exports food to many other Indian States.

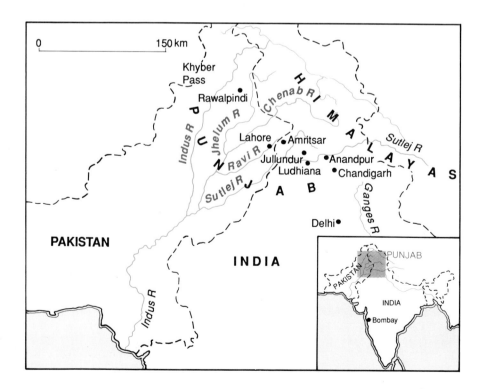

This is a map of the original Punjab. It is the "Land of Five Rivers" – which is what "Punjab" means.

The most famous and respected of all Sikh buildings – the Golden Temple in Amritsar

The Golden Temple

For Sikhs the **Golden Temple** is an important place of pilgrimage. They visit it from all over the Punjab and from wherever else in the world they have settled. Sikhs call the Golden Temple "Harimandir Sahib", which means the abode of God. It has four doors, one on each side, offering welcome to people from any direction.

Making a new home

Harminder Singh and his twin sisters, Amardeep Kaur and Kamaldeep Kaur, were born in Britain. Their father, Satwant Singh, was born in Uganda. He completed his secondary education in Kenya and came to England in 1968. After the necessary training, he took a job with British Telecom and settled in this country. Kawaljeet Kaur, their mother, was also born in Uganda. She went to India for further education and graduated in economics.

Satwant Singh has many friends in England and his family live here too. Kawaljeet Kaur left her parents in India to begin life as a married woman in a country totally strange to her. She describes what it was like coming to Britain:

> "It took me some time to get used to doing most of the housework myself, though my husband helped me sometimes. In my family men do not do womanly chores in the house. It was strange for me to mow the lawn because women don't do such work in India."

Living in Croydon, with no friends in the neighbourhood, Kawaljeet often felt depressed and longed to be back in the Punjab. Because of this Kawaljeet Kaur and Satwant Singh moved to Heston, Middlesex, to be near other Sikh families.

- Discuss why Harminder's parents came to Britain and how Harminder's mother felt when she first arrived. Put their thoughts and feelings into a poem about being a stranger.

Key Words
Punjab
Golden Temple

2 A special place

What makes a place special for us?

It may be the place we most enjoy being or where we meet people we like to be with. It could be home, our own room, a football stadium, a shop or café, a place in the countryside, beside the sea or in a town.

● Think of a place that is special for you and explain what it is like, where it is and why it is special. Share this with a partner.

Sometimes we make a place special by what we do there. For Sikhs, this is true of the **gurdwara**. A gurdwara is a Sikh place of worship and the place where Sikhs celebrate their festivals. The word means "House of God" or "at the Guru's door" (Guru means a religious teacher). Sikhs use the word **Guru** as a title before the name of each of their ten Gurus and before the name of their holy book, the **Guru Granth Sahib**.

What does a gurdwara look like?

● What differences do you notice between the buildings opposite? Look for something they have in common.

When Harminder went to India he noticed that the traditional design of the gurdwaras was very different from those in England. The domes, the use of marble, the white colour which gives the feeling of purity and calm to the place, and the open space surrounding the building, are missing in England. This is because in Britain, Canada and the USA buildings, such as houses or disused churches, have been converted to serve the purpose.

For any building to be called a gurdwara it must have a copy of the Guru Granth Sahib placed in a suitable room in the correct manner. (We shall learn more of this later.) A gurdwara must also have a large kitchen in which meals for the congregation can be cooked. There must also be a Sikh flag flying high outside the building. The flag is triangular in shape and yellowish orange in colour. It shows that the building belongs to Sikhs.

The flag is very important to Sikhs because the designs on it represent things which are important to them. In the middle of the flag is the sign called khanda. The sword on the right represents

Both pictures show a gurdwara. The one above is in India and the one opposite is in England – in Southampton.

guidance in religious matters and the one on the left guidance in worldly matters. The circle in the middle shows that all people are equal and that there is a balance between religious and worldly matters. The two-edged sword represents freedom and justice.

- Do you belong to a group or team which has a symbol on a badge or flag? Discuss its meaning. Devise a class or group symbol with a special meaning.

- Make a Sikh flag. Think about the shape and colour. What materials could you use? How could you show the symbols? Copy the khanda symbol on page 48.

Key Words

gurdwara Guru
Granth Sahib

3 Entering in

ਤਿੱਠ ਸਭੇ ਘ... ... ... ਤੁਧੁ ਜੋਹਿਆ

This picture is of the inside of the gurdwara that Harminder and his sisters attend in London.

● Describe the picture above in as much detail as you can. What are the most important or unusual things in the picture?

● Talk or write about the people. What are they doing and what are they wearing? What questions would you like to ask the people there? After deciding on your questions, see if any of them are answered in the explanation opposite.

Showing respect

Harminder explains how to behave when visiting a gurdwara:

> "Sikhs and any visitors to the gurdwara must remove their shoes before entering the prayer room. This is because shoes are considered unclean to take into the presence of our holy book, the Guru Granth Sahib. All except very young children must cover their head before going into the prayer room. Sikh men and boys wear a **turban**; women and girls use their **duppatta** – the long scarf they carry on their shoulders – to cover their heads. Visitors who are not Sikhs must also cover their heads. This is also done to show respect for our holy book."

As the Guru Granth Sahib is treated with great reverence by Sikhs it is kept higher than where people sit in the gurdwara. The holy book is placed on a miniature bed called Manji Sahib, which rests on the platform under a richly decorated canopy. Several sets of cloths are used to cover the Granth Sahib and the area around it. These cloths are called rumalas. On entering a gurdwara Sikhs walk straight to the Guru Granth Sahib, place an offering of money or food before it, bow down to it almost touching their forehead to the floor and then sit down on the floor facing the holy book with their legs crossed. They never sit with their back or their feet pointing towards the Guru Granth Sahib.

● What are the different ways in which Sikhs show respect in a gurdwara?
   — What are they showing respect to and why?
   — Can you think of times when you show respect in similar ways? For example, explain how you show respect when greeting a guest in your house or when going to someone else's house.
   — How else do *you* show respect to people or things?

Serving a community

Gurdwaras also act as community centres. They are used for teaching languages such as Punjabi and English, scriptures, hymn singing and playing musical instruments. Senior citizens, women and youth organisations also use gurdwara buildings for their activities.

Key Words

turban   duppatta

9

4 A precious possession

The Guru Granth Sahib

The Sikh community's most precious possession is their holy book, the Guru Granth Sahib. Look carefully at the picture below which shows the covered book under the canopy. Make a list of all the things you can see that you already know something about. Use your list to help you explain to a partner as much as you can about this picture.

● Think about what is your most precious possession. Why is it so precious to you? Make three rules about how you would like other people to treat this valuable object.

● What things does your family have that are of special value? Think of one of them and explain why it is so valuable.

The Guru Granth Sahib was compiled by **Guru Arjun**, the fifth Guru of the Sikhs. He included the writings of the first four Gurus, his own writings and those of Hindu and Muslim saints. Some of these saints belonged to the lower classes of the Indian society of the day. The Sikh Gurus preached that all human beings were created by the same God. Before Him the Hindu and the Muslim, the touchable and the untouchable ("clean" and "unclean" people), the high and the low were the same. Everyone was acceptable to God and could worship Him.

Guru Arjun called the book the **Adi Granth**, meaning the first great book. Guru Arjun paid his respects to the Adi Granth by always bowing to it, a tradition still followed today. He did this to show his followers that the teachings of God, or God's Word, is far more important than the human Guru.

The Granth Sahib contains **Gurbani** ("Guru's Word"). God revealed Bani (i.e. the Word) to the Gurus. Hence Gurbani is the divine Word that has come through the Gurus and, therefore, must be respected.

Guru **Gobind Singh**, the tenth Guru of the Sikhs, added his father's hymns to the Granth Sahib. In 1708, Guru Gobind Singh told his followers that the Granth Sahib was going to be the *living* spiritual teacher of the Sikhs. He also said that there would be no more human Gurus because he had completed the mission which Guru **Nanak** had begun. He too bowed to the holy book and since then it has become known as the Guru Granth Sahib.

Respect for the Guru Granth Sahib

The Guru Granth Sahib must be kept covered when not being read, to protect it from getting dirty. Anybody who wants to read it must cover his or her head and must wash their hands before touching its sacred pages. At night it is folded and put away in a separate room. If this is not possible, then the folded copy of the Guru Granth Sahib may be left under the canopy. Each morning before dawn the **Granthi** (the person who looks after the Guru Granth Sahib) must take a bath and dress in fresh clothes before opening the Book. The same would be done in a private home by someone who owned a copy of the holy book.

● The diagram below shows some of the main things you need to know about the Guru Granth Sahib. Use this information, in the order you think most important, to explain why the Guru Granth Sahib is so important to Sikhs. Compare your order with others in the class and discuss any differences.

Key Words

Arjun   Adi Granth
Gurbani   Gobind Singh
Nanak   Granthi

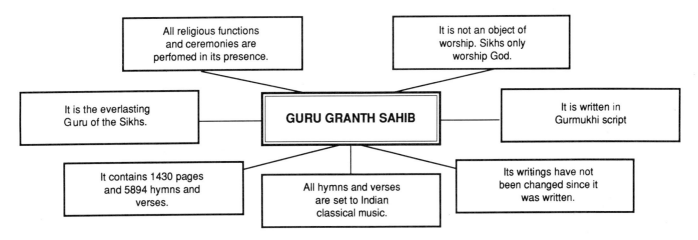

All religious functions and ceremonies are performed in its presence.

It is not an object of worship. Sikhs only worship God.

It is the everlasting Guru of the Sikhs.

GURU GRANTH SAHIB

It is written in Gurmukhi script

It contains 1430 pages and 5894 hymns and verses.

All hymns and verses are set to Indian classical music.

Its writings have not been changed since it was written.

5 Special celebrations

Birthday celebrations

- How do you celebrate birthdays in your family? You probably send cards, give gifts and have special food. In small groups, discuss what you do. Does your family have any custom that no one else has?

- Discuss what you think birthdays are for and think of a small ceremony to remember the "birthday" of your class.

Birthdays are usually a way of celebrating when we were born and who we are – though parents sometimes prefer to forget theirs! Other birthdays are different from this. In England, the Queen's birthday is a public event with more formal celebrations. She represents a whole nation and her official birthday celebrates that nation as well as her place at the head of it. Similarly, the birthday of Guru Nanak celebrates the birth of Sikhism and all that Sikhs stand for. Sikhs measure themselves against the standard set by their first Guru.

Gurpurbs

Guru Nanak's birthday is one of a number of Sikh festivals called **gurpurbs**. The word means a day celebrating the life of a guru. These celebrations take place in gurdwaras. Sikhs come together, often dressed in new and colourful clothes, in order to pray, read the Guru Granth Sahib and sing celebrational songs. These activities have special names. Here are some of them.

Every gurpurb begins with **Akhand Path**. This is a continuous reading of the Guru Granth Sahib, which starts early in the morning and lasts for 48 hours. It is done in two-hour relays. Each reader must have a bath and dress in clean clothes before his or her turn to read.

On the last day of the Akhand Path, people come to the gurdwara early in the morning to listen to the last few pages of the Guru Granth Sahib. Everybody listens quietly. In England, Sikh festivals are celebrated on a Sunday following the actual date; so in this country Akhand Path starts on a Friday morning and finishes on a Sunday morning. In India, Guru Nanak's birthday and all other gurpurbs are celebrated on the date they fall.

As the reading of the last page of the Guru Granth Sahib finishes, musicians known as ragis recite Anand Sahib, a hymn of joy by Guru Amar Das. The seated congregation join in with the ragis to

The Granthi reading from the Guru Granth Sahib.

recite the hymn. The ragis play Indian musical instruments such as the harmonium and the tabla. Anand Sahib is recited at the end of all Sikh ceremonies and all services.

As soon as the reciting of the Anand Sahib is finished, **Ardas** is offered. This formal prayer is led by the Granthi or a baptised Sikh woman or man. The congregation stands, facing the Guru Granth Sahib, with their hands folded and heads bent downwards in humility. The Ardas draws everyone's attention to the teachings of the Gurus, the sufferings and sacrifices of the Sikh martyrs and the words of the Guru Granth Sahib. At this point everybody bows down to the floor, touching their forehead to the ground and then stands up again. In the final part of the Ardas, God is asked to keep the Khalsa (the pure ones) faithful and to bless the whole of mankind. Everybody bows down to the ground once again before sitting down.

Once the Ardas is over, the Granthi reads **Hukumnamah**. This is God's guidance given by opening the Guru Granth Sahib at random and reading the first complete verse on the left-hand page. Many Sikhs who keep a copy of the Guru Granth Sahib at home, take Hukumnamah daily, particularly in the morning before beginning the day's work.

● Design and make a card to send to a Sikh friend as a greeting on Guru Nanak's birthday. Think carefully about what words you would choose to write inside.

Key Words

gurpurbs   Akhand Path
Ardas   Hukumnamah

6 Karah Parshad

What is Karah?

Karah is a dessert made from semolina or flour, ghee or butter, sugar and water. If you wish to make plain Karah more interesting you can add sultanas, raisins or currants, chopped almonds and cardamom seeds. When Karah is made to be served as a sacred food, the additional ingredients, such as sultanas, are not added.

What makes it Parshad?

Parshad means the food that has been blessed by first offering it to God. When Karah is made to be served as Parshad, certain other rules have to be followed. It can be made by men or women, but whoever makes it must bathe first, put on clean clothes and make sure that the kitchen and the utensils are clean. The person making Karah Parshad must remove their shoes outside the kitchen, keep their heads covered all the time and recite hymns during its preparation. When it is cooked, it should be covered with a clean white cloth and carried to the prayer room before it is time for Ardas. The person who makes the Karah Parshad carries it above their head and shoulders. Another person carries water in a clean container and sprinkles it all the way to the prayer room ahead of the person carrying the Karah Parshad. The sprinkling of water symbolises cleanliness. Inside the prayer room, the Karah Parshad is placed on a table which is kept on one side of the Guru Granth Sahib.

A volunteer washes his or her hands and stands near the Karah Parshad with a special sword called a **kirpan**. Towards the end of Ardas, at the utterance of specific words, the volunteer blesses the Karah Parshad by marking it with the kirpan.

Volunteers – both men and women – serve the Karah Parshad after the Granthi has read the Hukumnamah. These volunteers must not show any favouritism when distributing Karah Parshad. Those receiving it must not show any greed. Any one volunteer will first take out five portions in the name of the **Panj Pyare**, the original five men baptised by the tenth Guru, and will serve these portions to five Sikhs who live by the Sikh Code of Conduct. The rest of the congregation is served after this. Small amounts are put into the two hands cupped together and eaten straight away. Care should be taken not to waste a crumb because it is blessed food. The person who sits behind the Guru Granth Sahib has his share kept in a dish so that he can eat it when his duty is finished. The share for very small children is given to the parents. Sometimes people take small amounts of Karah Parshad home for family members who are unable to come to the gurdwara.

The serving and eating of Karah Parshad is a reminder of equality and unity within the Sikh community. As food it also reminds Sikhs of the common brotherhood of the people of the world and that in the presence of God no one should remain hungry.

How is it made?

Here is a recipe for a small amount of Karah. You can use a tea cup as a measure. It is important that you use the same cup to measure all the ingredients.

Now that you have read about Karah Parshad, look at this picture and explain as much as you can about what is happening and why.

1 level cupful of semolina
1 level cupful clarified butter (called ghee)
1 level cupful sugar
2 cupfuls water

Prepare the syrup by boiling sugar and water until the sugar is dissolved. Remove from the heat. Then place the ghee and semolina in a saucepan or Indian krahi or Chinese wok and cook on medium heat. Stir all the time until golden brown. Add the syrup and continue stirring until all the water is absorbed and the mixture blends together. The cooked mixture will be thick and slightly oily. Serve hot or warm.

7 Food for the soul

The atmosphere during a gurpurb is very relaxed. People come and go throughout the celebrations, which last until afternoon. After Karah Parshad is served, they take turns to go to the dining hall to eat breakfast but others stay on to listen to the **Asa di Var**. This is a collection of hymns composed by Guru Nanak himself. They are also sung daily in all gurdwaras before sunrise and some Sikh families invite musicians to their homes especially to sing these hymns.

Experienced ragis are able to create a special atmosphere when singing hymns. To the Sikhs this is a way of worshipping God. Ragis often encourage the congregation to sing with them. This is called **kirtan**. Those who do it and those who listen to it hope to be drawn towards God. The Gurus say that kirtan is food for the soul.

Ragis performing in a gurdwara in London.

- Look at the picture. Study the instruments and faces carefully and explain what sort of music you think the ragis are playing.

- What music do you like to listen to and how does it make you feel? Discuss this with a partner.

- Think of music that makes you feel sad, happy, excited and peaceful. Try to give one example of each of these and play it to your class.

The power of kirtan

There is a story about Guru Nanak and his lifelong companion Bhai Mardana who always played rabaab, a sort of violin, when he sang with the Guru. During their travels they stayed with a friend in Eminabad (now in Pakistan). This town was under attack from Baber, a strong ruler who wanted to be emperor of India. He entered the town and put Guru Nanak and Bhai Mardana in jail along with many other innocent men, women and children. Conditions were wretched and miserable. To help them, Nanak sang songs in praise of God. The power of this kirtan calmed them and helped them forget their pain.

Another time, when Guru Nanak and other prisoners were grinding corn with handmills, he started to sing devotional songs to bring some happiness to them all. While listening to Guru Nanak the prisoners forgot to grind the corn – yet the handmills continued to work on their own! This amazed not only the prisoners and prison officer but also Baber himself who agreed to free the prisoners on the advice of the Guru.

When the Guru settled down in Kartarpur, after his travels, his daily routine began three hours before dawn. This time is very peaceful and is a good time to sing the sacred hymns and remember God.

- Listen to a kirtan session on a record or tape. Why do you think Sikhs find this music peaceful and inspiring? List three reasons and share them.

Many Sikh children go to classes in gurdwaras to learn kirtan and during gurpurbs they sing before the congregation. On the next page you can read about a girl and her friends who do just this.

Key Words   Asa di Var   kirtan

---

8 Making music together

Here is a picture of a group of young Sikhs who play kirtan. Below is a description of what they do, written by Gopinder Kaur. She is playing the harmonium in the picture.

"I belong to a group of young Sikhs who learn and perform kirtan – singing hymns from the Guru Granth Sahib.

"We have classes every Sunday where, as well as singing, we learn how to play the vaja, or harmonium. The shabads (hymns) we sing are accompanied by the tabla, or drums. The tabla itself is a very difficult instrument to master. Most of us have been learning kirtan for about two years, and we have now formed ourselves into a jatha, or group. We perform kirtan in the gurdwara, especially on important occasions such as gur-purbs. We are often invited to people's houses when they wish to have a kirtan programme. We even perform instead of the professional ragis.

"In a gurdwara we sit in front of the **sangat**, or congregation, near the Guru Granth Sahib. By now we have all gained in confidence and become more experienced in singing in front of a large congregation. We have lost our initial "stage fright". This is because singing kirtan is not a "solo performance", but something in which everybody participates.

"So, how does kirtan differ from singing any other song? The words you sing are from the Guru Granth Sahib. They should be sung in an attitude of prayer and meditation, so that there is something beyond the pleasing melody. Firstly, as the sangat sings, the vibrations coming from within us and around us have a physical effect on the body. As you become more and more absorbed in the words you sing, you become less self-conscious. The cares of everyday life, which dominate our thoughts so much, begin to disappear. It is very rare for our minds to be completely released from worldly cares, but kirtan is one way of doing this.

In these ways, kirtan can be soothing, refreshing and uplifting. It leaves us in a state of peace and turns our minds directly and completely to God. Kirtan is therefore a way to experience God.

For our jatha, there is another benefit in performing kirtan: it brings blessings and good wishes from the sangat, so the fact that people have appreciated our kirtan makes us want to continue learning.

Questions

- What questions would you like to ask Gopinder and her group about the music they play and the songs they sing?

- Is there anything that you do that is very important to you? Explain how it is different from or similar to Gopinder learning kirtan.

 **Key Word**

sangat

9 Guru Nanak's childhood

On Guru Nanak's birthday Sikhs remember him as the Messenger of God. So when they are gathered in gurdwaras, they listen to sermons, talks, ballads and poetry – all on Guru Nanak's life. Here are a few of the stories they hear.

Mysteries

Guru Nanak's childhood was full of mysteries. He was a real worry to his father. Strange things happened around him. For example, he was seen asleep on the grass with a large cobra shading his face from the sun with its hood. Another time he was seen resting in the shade of a tree. The shadow of this tree stayed over him, whilst the shadows of other trees moved with the sun. On another occasion, while he sat praying, his father's cows which he took to graze went into a farmer's field and destroyed the crop. When the farmer complained to his father, Guru Nanak told him to go back and look again. When he did, there was no damage done.

Gurdwara Kiara Sahib

A gurdwara called Kiara Sahib now stands in this field.

- Imagine you are a guide who has brought some people to this special place. Explain why it is so important for Sikhs, how it shows that Nanak was an unusual child and why a gurdwara was built there.

Trading money for a blessing

੧ਓ IK ONKAAR	There is One God
ਸਤਿਨਾਮੁ SAT NAAM	God's name is Truth
ਕਰਤਾਪੁਰਖੁ KARTA PURKH	God is the Creator
ਨਿਰਭਉ NIR BHAU	God is without Fear
ਨਿਰਵੈਰੁ NIR VAIR	God is without Hate
ਅਕਾਲ ਮੂਰਤਿ AKAAL MOORAT	God is Immortal
ਅਜੂਨੀ AJOONI	God is beyond Birth and Death
ਸੈਭੰ SAIBHANG	God is Self-Illuminated
ਗੁਰ ਪ੍ਰਸਾਦਿ ॥ GUR PARSAAD	God is realised by the Grace of the Guru

The Mool Mantar

Mool Mantar

In India at this time there were many holy men who left their homes and travelled, living off what others gave them, while they searched for God. Nanak enjoyed the company of these men. He was once spanked by his father for spending money on feeding a group of them who were hungry. To young Nanak they were men of God, not beggars as his father thought. The money had been given to Nanak for buying goods–not food–because his father wanted to set him up in business. Nanak thought he traded his money well because those few rupees earned him the blessings of the holy men

- Imagine the conversation between Nanak and his father about what he had done. With a partner, argue why Nanak thought he had done well and why his father thought he had done badly.

To calm the situation between Nanak and his father, his only sister, Nanaki, took him to Sultanpur. She set him up in a job with her husband, Jai Ram, who worked for a nawab (Indian noble man). Nanaki loved her brother and was the first to recognise his greatness. In Sultanpur Nanak used to get up hours before dawn, bathe in a river and meditate, before starting work. He used to tell people that to be happy they should earn their living honestly, share with others and remember God all the time.

- What do you think of Nanak's message? Can you remember a time when not being honest or not sharing has made you unhappy? Discuss this together.

One morning Guru Nanak simply disappeared from the bank of the river where he was always seen. His clothes were there, but where was he? People thought he was drowned. Only his sister Nanaki was sure her brother was safe. After three days, Guru Nanak reappeared. He remained silent for a day. The next day he broke his silence by saying that there was only one way to God, whatever faith you belonged to. It is said that during the time he was missing, he had a vision of God whom he described in the words on the left.

Guru Nanak's description of God is called **Mool Mantar**. Every Sikh is expected to recite it daily. These words are so important to Sikhs that the Guru Granth Sahib begins with them.

10 Guru Nanak's travels

The four great journeys of Guru Nanak

His vision of God changed Nanak's life. He gave up his work as a storekeeper to spread God's message of love, peace and truth to the peoples of the world. He gave his possessions to the poor and set off with two friends, Bala and Mardana, on a long trek.

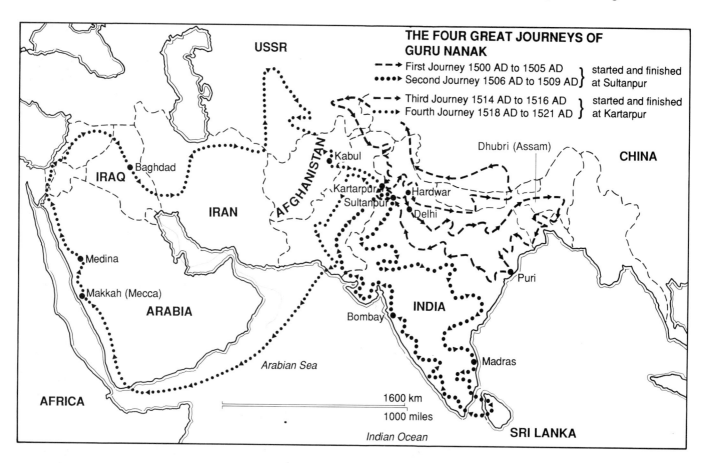

THE FOUR GREAT JOURNEYS OF GURU NANAK
- – – ▶ First Journey 1500 AD to 1505 AD } started and finished at Sultanpur
- • • • ▶ Second Journey 1506 AD to 1509 AD } started and finished at Sultanpur
- – – ▶ Third Journey 1514 AD to 1516 AD } started and finished at Kartarpur
- • • • ▶ Fourth Journey 1518 AD to 1521 AD } started and finished at Kartarpur

- Look at the map. Study the plotting of the four great journeys Guru Nanak undertook. Taking Kartarpur and Sultanpur as the starting and returning points, write down the direction of each journey and the names of places through which he travelled. Can you estimate the total number of miles?

- Has anything happened to you that has changed the way you think or live? Perhaps it was going to school or making new friends. How were things different? Think of two or three ways in which your life changed.

Guru Nanak visited almost every holy place of the Hindus, the Muslims and the Buddhists, spending a total of 22 years meeting people and spreading his message of goodwill. Nanak believed that people should not go to far-off, lonely places to show their love for God. In order to be useful to people and do good for them we must live with them. Here are two stories that show what this means.

Sajjan the robber

During his travels Guru Nanak heard of Sajjan the robber. He decided to visit this robber. When Sajjan heard Guru Nanak's songs of devotion to God and his teachings, he was so impressed that he gave up robbing and killing people who stayed at his guest house. Sajjan felt very ashamed of his activities. He confessed his crimes to the Guru and prayed to God for His forgiveness. Nanak told Sajjan to distribute all his ill-earned wealth to the needy and the poor. Sajjan became Guru Nanak's follower. It is said that the first Sikh temple was built by Sajjan on the spot where he changed from an evil to a good man.

● One of Guru Nanak's sayings was "A man becomes good in the company of the good". How do you think the story of Sajjan the robber puts this saying into practice?

Mardana's thirst

Once during their travels Nanak's companion, Mardana, was very thirsty. At the request of Guru Nanak he went to Wali Kandhari, a Muslim saint, for a drink of water. Mardana was refused a drink repeatedly. The fourth time he was told that "If your Guru is so great, he should provide you with water". Guru Nanak asked Mardana to dig a hole on the side of the hill where they were resting. At first the water came in small amounts. Then it gushed out. The reservoir of water on the hill top where Wali lived began to dry up. Wali was furious. He rolled down a boulder to kill Mardana. Guru Nanak raised his hand. Miraculously, the boulder stopped. Guru Nanak's hand left an imprint on it which is still there today. Wali accepted Guru Nanak's greatness and became his devotee (follower). A gurdwara marks this spot. Many people go to Hasan Abdal in Pakistan to see the shrine of Guru Nanak's hand imprint and the pool of water which gushed out under the boulder, which stands as the living miracle.

● Imagine you are a guide standing at this spot with a group of travellers. Explain, in your own words, why the hand imprint is there and what this story is meant to show about Guru Nanak. These words may help: protect, bless, give life.

11 Guru Nanak's message

Gopinder and her sisters admiring a picture of Guru Nanak by a famous Sikh artist, Sobha Singh.

What was he like?

- Look at the picture closely. What qualities of Guru Nanak do you think the artist wanted to show us in his painting? Try to write at least five words that describe the Guru.

Another way in which we can discover what Guru Nanak was like and what he thought is through his prayers and hymns. The most important thing in life for Guru Nanak was to know what God wanted him to do. He felt that the thing everyone should search for was to know God's will. He wrote this down many times in his meditations. Here are two examples:

"What He wills He ordains
To Him no one can give an order
For He, O Nanak, is the King of Kings
As He wills so we must live."

> "Abide by His will and make it your own
> His will, O Nanak, that is written in your heart."

How do you know God's will? This is a diffcult question. There are many hurdles that stand in our way, possibly stopping us from reaching God: wealth, power, beauty, self-importance and many other temptations. If you are to reach God you must surrender unconditionally to His will. Nanak told these stories to show what this means:

Duni Chand and his riches

On his travels, Guru Nanak arrived one day near Lahore. Guru Nanak was visited by Duni Chand and his wife. Duni Chand had an enormous fortune and lived very comfortably. Despite his wealth, his continuous desire to get richer had made Duni Chand very unhappy. He invited Guru Nanak to his house. Before leaving Duni Chand's house, Guru Nanak gave him a needle. He asked Duni Chand to keep it safe and to give it back to him when he asks for it in the next world. "But how can one carry a needle to the next world?" asked Duni Chand.

"Then what have you collected all these riches for?" asked Guru Nanak.

When Duni Chand and his wife heard this, they fell at Nanak's feet. Duni Chand became a changed person and gave all his wealth to the poor. He gave in to the will of God and started sharing his earnings with the needy.

Truthful living

For Guru Nanak another way of following the will of God was truthful living.

After his travels Guru Nanak returned and settled in Kartarpur, where he spent the next 18 years living with his family and his followers. He continued to remind them that, "Truth is High, but Higher still is truthful living."

● Explain in your own words three things you have read about Guru Nanak which are examples of this saying.

● Discuss in groups or with a partner what sort of a man you think Guru Nanak was. Try to agree on three special qualities he had. Briefly describe his character.

● Explain what you think are the three most special qualities you look for in another person.

12 Langar

When Guru Nanak had settled down in Kartarpur people from all walks of life came to listen to his devotional songs and his talks about life and religion. There were Muslims, there were Hindus, there were those of high caste and low caste*, and there were rich and poor gathered around him. They all cooked and ate food together and this was the beginning of **Guru Ka Langar**, the sharing of food among the faithful.

Later on, **Guru Amar Das** ordered that all those who wished to meet him must first eat langar in the Guru's kitchen. Even Akbar, the Emperor of India, had to sit on the floor side by side with the ordinary people to eat his langar, before he could see Guru Amar Das.

During the days of **Guru Ram Das**, meals were served to travellers and squatters too. If you read the history of the Sikh Gurus, you will find many more examples of Gurus serving langar to one and all.

Today langar is served during the gurpurb and at the end of every service at a gurdwara. During a gurpurb, whilst most members of the congregation are listening to the praises of Guru Nanak in the prayer hall, there are others – men and women, boys and girls – who are busy preparing and cooking food for the congregation and anybody else who may call at the gurdwara.

Blessing the langar

A little of each item of food to be served in the langar is put on a plate. It is covered, taken into the prayer room and placed in front of the Guru Granth Sahib, near the Karah Parshad. Langar is blessed with a kirpan during Ardas at the same time as the Karah Parshad, by the same volunteer. The blessed food is taken back to the kitchen and mixed with the remaining food of its own kind. This blesses the entire langar. During gurpurb in bigger gurdwaras, langar is blessed in the kitchen before the service ends. This is so that the serving of it can be started earlier for the children and their mothers and to cope with large numbers of people.

Langar is always strictly vegetarian. So the cooking of meat, fish, and eggs, and the serving of alcohol, is totally forbidden in the gurdwaras – as is smoking. Whether Sikhs should be vegetarians or non-vegetarians is a personal matter. However, those who eat meat will avoid eating beef and other meat which is prepared by

* Caste means a large group of families whose ancestors shared the same occupation. Members of a caste may trace their ancestry back to the same important person. High caste means those with "important" jobs and a rich background. Low caste refers to those who do more menial jobs, such as working in the fields, carpentry, making pots or serving high caste families.

the ritual killing of an animal. It is said that the food we eat affects both body and mind.

- Look carefully at the picture. Describe what you see.

- Guru Nanak's advice to his followers was:
  "Do not eat or drink that food which may cause pain and suffering to the body or mind." What do you think he meant by that? Give some examples.

- If you were asked to cook a meal for a Sikh friend following the rules of langar what would you cook and why?

- Think of any special foods that you eat at a particular time: on Sundays, at Christmas or perhaps when you go out somewhere like to the seaside or the fair. What are these foods and why do you think you eat them?

Paying for langar

Every Sikh is expected to pay a tenth of their income for the community's welfare, some of which is used to run the community kitchens in the gurdwaras. Often whole families take turns to pay for langar. Every Sikh feels honoured to contribute – cooking and serving langar and even washing up dirty dishes! This is an act of charity and service. In most gurdwaras, particularly those in India, langar is served daily, day and night. In this way, langar remains as important a part of the Sikh way of life as it was during the time of the Gurus.

Key Words

Guru Ka Langar
Guru Amar Das
Ram Das

13 A sad victory

The martydom of Guru Arjun Dev

The gurpurb celebrated in honour of Guru Arjun's martyrdom is called "Guru Arjun Dev ji da Shahidi Gurpurb". **Shahidi** means martyrdom. At the shahidi gurpurb the Sikhs mourn the death of their fifth Guru.

Arjun Dev

What led to his death?

Emperor Jahangir came to the throne in 1605. Guru Arjun Dev had been carrying on his work since 1581; that is, for over 24 years. He was very successful but this meant he had made many enemies. Above all, many Muslims were furious that he should offer people a different faith to their own. Now and again they would meet the Emperor and complain to him about the Guru. They said, "In Goindwal (on the bank of the river Beas in the Punjab) there is a religious teacher named Arjun. He is looked upon as a holy saint and has many followers. He preaches a religion called Sikhism which is against Islam. He has become very popular and crowds of people flock to him. Worst of all, many Muslims become his followers and more and more are doing so every day. All this is happening in the empire of a Muslim emperor! It is very sad and it is your duty to stop this."

Emperor Jahangir agreed with them. Having made up his mind to convert or kill Guru Arjun Dev, Emperor Jahangir was on the look out for a suitable chance or excuse to carry this out.

The chance came to him about six months later.

How was he killed?

It was May, when temperatures can rise up to 60°C (120°F). Guru Arjun had been captured. He was first denied food and water. Then he was put in a large vessel of boiling water and burning sand was poured over his head. After this, he was made to sit over an iron plate heated from below and once again hot burning sand was poured over his head and body from above. Throughout this ordeal Guru Arjun remained calm. He simply said, "It is the Will of God and we have to let it happen His way. Forgiveness is better than revenge. Suffering gives strength to the cause of Truth."

After his death

At the Guru's request, his burnt and blistered body was finally taken to be bathed in the river Ravi, where it disappeared and, Sikhs believe, became one with God. The Gurdwara Dehra Sahib in Lahore now stands as a reminder of this first martyred Guru. To remember that he was denied water for three days before being tortured to death, the Sikhs serve free soft drinks, cold water and **sharbat** from a **shabeel** on every road to passers by all day during the gurpurb. Guru Arjun gave the Sikhs the Guru Granth Sahib, and in following the teachings contained in it he gave his life. This gurpurb celebrates the sacrifice he made as a great victory.

- Explain why Sikhs think of Guru Arjun's death as a great victory. Discuss this carefully with a partner.

- What else could Guru Arjun have done in this situation? Why did he behave as he did? Discuss these questions together.

- Study the picture of Arjun Dev carefully. Why do you think the artist has painted him in this way? Would you have painted a similar or a different picture?

Key Words

Shahidi   sharbat
shabeel

14   Selfless service

- Look at this picture of Guru **Teg Bahadur**. What qualities do you think the artist was trying to show the Guru had? Read on and see whether this story suggests the same qualities.

The martyrdom of Guru Teg Bahadur

During the lunar month of Maghar (which comes during November and December), Sikhs remember the death of their ninth guru, Teg Bahadur. In Delhi, the capital city of India, there is a gurdwara called Sis Ganji where you can see the preserved tree under which Guru Teg Bahadur was beheaded.

Teg Bahadur lived at a time when Hindus in India were being persecuted by the Moslem emperor Aurangzeb. The emperor had become ruler by killing his brothers and his own father. He wished to convert everyone to Islam. A group of Hindu priests, called **pundits**, travelled all the way from Kashmir in the north to see the Guru in Anandpur for his advice. While they were wrestling with how to solve this grim problem, the Guru's nine-year-old son, **Gobind Rai** saw how worried his father was and asked what was bothering him. Teg Bahadur explained the problem of the Hindus in Kashmir and how they must either convert to Islam or be persecuted. He told his son the only solution he could think of: "They can be saved only if a great man can offer himself in their place."

"But who is greater than you?" his proud son replied.

This convinced the Guru of what he must do. "Tell your tormentors," he said, "that you will be willing to accept Islam if Guru Teg Bahadur can first be persuaded to do so."

Teg Bahadur knew he must prepare for the task carefully and that he did not have long. With him went a few of his followers. When they reached the palace in Agra, officials came and arrested them. Teg Bahadur was chained and imprisoned in an iron cage. First they tried to tempt him to accept the Islamic faith. When this did not work the emperor said, "If you are a man of God, you must save yourself by working a miracle."

The Guru said, "There is no place for miracles in a true religion. No holy man will perform miracles to prove his greatness."

To try and change his mind four of his disciples were killed before his eyes. Teg Bahadur was not moved. He understood this to be the will of God and now it was his turn. He was allowed to bathe at a nearby well. Then he was told to sit under a banyan tree on a platform. Crowds of people had gathered to see the execution. The Guru told his executioner: "When I bow to God, at the end of my prayers, behead me." The executioner did exactly that on 11 November 1675.

God's will

- Doing God's will is very important for Sikhs. A Sikh believes that by living in harmony with the Will of God and his own will, he brings peace for himself. What examples of this can you find in the story? In pairs or small groups, take one of these examples and think about what difficulties Teg Bahadur may have faced in making his decision.

- Why do you think Guru Teg Bahadur's martyrdom is particularly special to Sikhs?

15 Sewa

Celebrating gurpurbs brings a feeling of togetherness, and a wish to serve the community and society at large. This selfless service is called **sewa** and must be done without any payment or expected reward. It has become an important part of the Sikh way of life and it can be offered in different ways according to the need. Doing any kind of sewa is good whether it is giving time, effort or money, working with your hands or your mind. It is your devotion and commitment that really matters. It is not only a way of helping others but also a way of coming closer to God.

● In what ways do you think you can best help your family, community or school? What are the jobs that you think need to be done? How could you or your class help with them?

Sukhbir Singh does sewa

"My name is Sukhbir Singh. My friend Manjit Singh and I usually go to our local gurdwara early in the morning on the day of the gurpurb. We are both 12 years old. A person doing sewa is called sewadar or sewak. We are given an armband each with 'sewadar' on it. In the mornings, some sewadars prepare pakoras (savoury fritters) and tea for breakfast; others cook langar – so there is always plenty of washing up to do. Manjit and I work as a team. There can be heavy things such as very large pans to carry from one place to another. There is always work in the dining room. After breakfast it needs to be cleaned to clear up any spilled food and prepared for serving langar. Manjit and I roll out and lay the long narrow mats in rows on the floor. People sit on these mats to eat langar. Later we collect dirty dishes and take them to the washing-up room. We do any work given to us. Sometimes we look after the shoes of the congregation; other times we sweep floors."

Why does Sukhbir Singh do sewa?

"Serving others gives me joy. I see the rich and the not-so-rich, the educated and the not-so-educated getting to know one another by doing sewa together. Sewa teaches me self-discipline because I have to sacrifice some other pleasures for it."

Girls and adult volunteers helping in a gurdwara kitchen.

Why does Manjit Singh do sewa?

"I think the very best way to know God is to serve his people. Though I'm still very young, I know I have to be very tolerant and respectful to other sewadars whose ways of doing things are different from mine. It helps me learn how to be humble."

- What do you think Manjit means when he says "It helps me learn how to be humble"?

- Would you be happy to do the jobs Sukhbir and Manjit were doing? Think of the jobs you find it difficult to make yourself do and explain the reasons why to a partner.

Serving others

For Sikhs the Gurus themselves set a perfect example of service. Angad, the second Guru, was chosen to be Guru because he was always ready to do any task, any number of times and at any time for Guru Nanak. For 12 years Amar Das brought firewood from the forest, helped with the cooking and serving of langar, did washing up and whatever else was asked of him. He also fetched water for Guru Angad's bath every morning. Eventually he became a Guru himself. Guru Arjun opened up a place for lepers in Tarn Taran in the Punjab. He also opened dispensaries in many places to look after the sick and the disabled. Today in India and in some other countries, Sikhs have opened many hospitals, orphanages, schools, colleges and other similar sorts of organisations.

Key Word

sewa

16 Guru Gobind Singh's birthday

Satpal Singh Sandhu, born in Uganda but brought up in Amritsar, says:

"In England, gurpurbs are not celebrated with the same pomp and ceremony as in India. Sikh children outside India miss out on a great deal of fun and enjoyment, particularly so on the gurpurb of Guru Gobind Singh's birthday. Sikhs organise processions through towns and cities. These processions are very colourful and the Guru Granth Sahib is carried on a decorated float with the Panj Pyare leading the float and the rest of the procession. The band plays music to the tune of hymns from the Guru Granth Sahib. Children taking part in the procession show off their banners bearing the names of their schools or other organisations. The spectators line the streets several rows deep. This lifts the spirits of the people who take part in the procession as they remember the birth of their tenth and last human Guru."

The Guru who was a soldier

Guru Gobind Singh's early childhood was spent with his mother and grandmother (his father's mother) in Patna. During this time his father, Guru Teg Bahadur, was preaching the Sikh faith in the eastern parts of India. In fact, Guru Gobind Singh's father was not in Patna when he was born. The family later joined Guru Teg Bahadur in Anandpur, where they lived with relatives and other devotees of the Guru. As a child his favourite sport was "mock battles" and he received training in archery, horse riding and the use of arms. At the age of nine the young Gobind became Guru, after his father's execution.

For safety, Guru Gobind Singh and his close followers moved from Anandpur to Paonta, a quiet place in the foothills near the river Jamuna. He studied the lives of the Gurus before him. He found how his grandfather, the sixth Guru, had to take up arms in defence of his home and faith. As he became more and more aware of the danger to him and his people, his earlier interest in mock battles turned into organised training in warfare. He said, "I must prepare an army that will destroy evil and tear out tyranny by its roots." His fight was not against any one religion; it was against tyranny and oppression.

The Soldier Saint

On his birthday, the congregation sits quietly in the gurdwara and listens to speakers telling stories about the life of Guru Gobind Singh. During the many battles against the Indian Rajas and the Moghals (Islamic rulers), he lost his two younger sons – Ajit Singh and Jujhar Singh – because they refused to give up their faith. They were bricked alive into a wall. The Guru's two older sons – Zorawar Singh and Fateh Singh – died on a battle-field along with many other followers of their father. Guru Gobind Singh's mother died too when she heard of her grandsons' deaths.

Guru Gobind Singh is always spoken of as the "Saint Soldier". When he was living at Paonta he often left his friends and went away alone to be with his heavenly father. He reminded people that "only those who love God's creation will find Him". Guru Gobind Singh was very fond of a Sikh named Kanhaiya. During the battles with the Moghals, Kanhaiya looked after the wounded. Some of the Sikhs fighting in the wars did not like the fact that Kanhaiya helped the enemy wounded as well. They complained to the Guru that Kanhaiya was a traitor. Guru Gobind Singh's response was to give Kanhaiya more ointment to apply to the wounds. The Guru told him, "You are a true Sikh of mine. Carry on with the good work. God will be highly pleased with you."

● Is it right to fight against what you think is evil? If you were talking to Guru Gobind Singh, what questions would you want to ask him about what he did?

17   Holla Maholla

Attack and counter-attack

Look at the picture above. It is a sword fight staged during the Sikh festival of Hola Maholla. The name of the festival actually means "attack and counter-attack". It may seem strange to stage battles during a religious festival. Why do you think Sikhs do this? (Look at pages 34–35 and 38–39 and read about Guru Gobind Singh. This will give you some clues.)

Every year Sikhs gather at a town called Anandpur on the day of Holi, the Hindu festival of colours. As well as mock battles, they stage military exercises and have horse riding and athletics contests in memory of Guru Gobind Singh and his followers. It was Guru Gobind Singh who called the occasion **Hola Maholla** and introduced these martial arts to shake the people out of their helplessness and give them back their dignity.

The most exciting thing about Hola Maholla is that it is impossible to watch what is happening without wanting to join in! It is full of activities in which the contestants show their skill with swords, bows and in hand-to-hand wrestling. Because the occasion is also a fair for everyone to enjoy, children can play their own traditional games. Here is one of them called Kabaddi. These are the rules.

"Kabaddi, Kabaddi!"

Divide the players into two groups. The teams stand facing each other with a line drawn down the centre. One person from the first team runs across to the other shouting "Kabaddi, Kabaddi!". He or she has to touch a member of the opposite team and run safely back to their own side. *But* the person must do this taking only *one* breath. If the person manages this then the person he or she touched is out of the game.

The other team must try and keep him or her on their side of the line until the person's breath runs out. If they do this he or she is out instead. A member of each team does this in turn until one team has no one left.

- Think up your own game called "Attack and counter-attack" to show some of the skills and qualities Sikhs admire.

- Have you ever watched an event you would really like to have taken part in – perhaps a football match, play or procession? Was there a person involved whose skills you admired? Discuss with a partner the event and the person. Say what it was that made them so exciting and try to convey this excitement to your partner in your description.

Colourful fairs

Folk arts have flourished in the Punjab. You can find them at festivals like Hola Maholla. Pottery, painting and wood carving are common examples; but two special ones are *phulkari*, which is embroidery, using designs based on flowers or shapes, and puppetry. Puppet shows are often held at night to create an exciting atmosphere. The puppets often represent well-known heroes and heroines.

Key Words

Hola Maholla

- Divide into groups and choose from the activities above connected with the Hola Maholla festival and traditional Punjabi fairs. Together create your own class festival fair based on this theme. You could use this for a class assembly to show the rest of your school.

18 Vaisakhi

The birth of the Khalsa, popularly known as Vaisakhi, is the most joyful Sikh festival. The festival marks the new year, celebrated on 13 April, as well as the tradition of initiating Sikhs into the Khalsa Panth or Brotherhood.

bhangra – a Punjabi folk dance

New year

In the Punjab the wheat harvest begins at the start of Vaisakh, the second month of the Indian calendar. Men, women and children dress in new, colourful clothes. Apart from going to gurdwaras, the Sikhs also get together on village commons and in community halls to celebrate the new year. Punjabi folk dances, particularly two called bhangra and gidha, are very popular forms of entertainment at these gatherings. Bhangra is performed by men and women together; gidha is a dance only for women.

- Look at the picture. What sort of dance do you think it is? In what ways does it suggest the new year?

- In small groups think about what sort of dance you would create to perform at New Year. What movements and music would it have? Try to perform a part of it.

Miracle or spectacle?

On Vaisakhi day as far back as 1699, thousands of followers of Guru Gobind Singh came to Anandpur. They came at the Guru's invitation to celebrate Vaisakhi. He appeared before them carrying a shining sword. Raising it up high, he made an alarming request. He asked, "Is there any one among you who will give his head to me to prove his faith in me?" Despite the fear this caused among the people, a man named Daya Ram stood up and offered his head. The Guru took him into a nearby tent and returned with his sword dripping with blood. He repeated his call for another head. The second Sikh who came forward was a farmer named Dharam Das. This amazing call for the sacrifice of a head was repeated five times. The third Sikh to respond to his Guru's call was Mohkam Chand, a washerman. A barber named Sahib Chand was the fourth person and Himmat Rai, a water carrier, was the fifth person.

While the people were wondering who was going to be next, everyone was stunned to see the Guru return with the five men alive and unharmed, dressed in saffron coloured clothes like his own. On seeing this breathtaking spectacle, the people were convinced that Guru Gobind Singh had performed a miracle by bringing the five back to life. The Guru announced to the congregation, "These are my Five Chosen Ones. Their spirit shall be part of my body and spirit, and mine shall be theirs." These men, who had passed the toughest of tests, were then initiated by Guru Gobind Singh. In turn, they initiated the Guru in the same way as he had done to them, upon his request. The five men, called Panj Pyare, were the beginning of the Khalsa Brotherhood – free of caste or other social differences. The Panj Pyare today initiate people in the same way.

- Why do you think Guru Gobind Singh chose his new brotherhood in this way? List three important qualities he was looking for in its members.

- Why do you think Sikhs might have needed this new brotherhood? You can look back at pages 34–35 for clues.

19

The birth of the Khalsa

Preparing amrit

Amrit is the baptismal water used to initiate Sikhs into the Khalsa. To do this, they must have a bath and dress in ceremonial robes. They wear blue or orange turbans and knee-length, saffron coloured tunics with a blue or orange sash over the shoulder and round the waist. They put fresh water in a steel bowl. They stir in patasas, a kind of puffed sugar cake, using a double-edged steel sword called a khanda – the type you see in the middle of the sign on a Sikh flag (see page 6). The steel bowl and steel sword represent strength and firmness. Water is used because it is the source of life; it purifies and cleans the body and brings back freshness. Also, when water has been blessed with prayers, Sikhs believe it cleanses the soul. When Guru Gobind Singh prepared the amrit, his wife added patasas to the water to show that the amrit was not only a sweet drink but also one which brought grace, tenderness and compassion.

Any five initiated Sikhs who keep strictly to the Sikh Code of Conduct can act as Panj Pyare and prepare amrit. They sit round in a circle resting on the right knee with both hands on the edge of the bowl, when preparing it. They recite five different prayers during the preparation. The sitting position shows that they are alert and ready to take action when needed.

● Read through the above passage again and pick out the qualities that a member of the Khalsa should have. Discuss these together.

Valjinder Singh and his wife were recently initiated into the Khalsa. Valjinder Singh explains why he took amrit:

"The moment I was waiting for came during the Vaisakhi gurpurb of 1987. My wife and I went to the gurdwara in Shepherd's Bush in London for the initiation. I was very excited but also a little apprehensive because I didn't know whether I would be able to keep to the expected discipline. I prayed to the Lord for His blessing and strength.

"My wife and I got ready and went to the gurdwara. The amrit was being prepared in the presence of the Guru Granth Sahib. This took almost an hour. I felt very happy and relaxed. I also became emotional, tears flowing from my eyes. I felt as if I was

A young man being baptised.

constantly being drawn towards some super power. I sat and waited with my eyes closed most of the time. When the amrit was ready, I opened my eyes. Physically, I felt very light as if I had just dropped down from the heavens. I drank the amrit each of the five times it was poured into my cupped hands. It was sprinkled five times into my eyes and five times into my hair. Each time I received amrit I had to say 'Wahe Guru ji ka Khalsa, Wahe Guru ji ki Fateh' meaning 'the Khalsa belongs to God and Victory be to Almighty God'. The Sikh Code of Conduct was once again explained to us. The ceremony ended with the reading of Anand Sahib, followed by Ardas and Hukumnamah. Karah Parshad was served to all.

"After taking amrit my faith in God has become almost complete. I now feel nothing belongs to me, everything belongs to my Guru."

Key Word

amrit

● What questions would you like to ask Valjinder Singh after reading about his initiation? What part of his description did you find the most important? Discuss these questions.

20 A code to live by

- Imagine you are starting a new community. In small groups, work out five rules or principles to live by and five ways to remember these rules day by day.

  When you have worked these out share them with the class. Which rules do you think are the best? What difficulties did you have making the rules and deciding how to remember them?

Faith in God

Guru Gobind Singh faced this problem when he initiated the Panj Pyare (see page 14) and ordered them to keep and to wear five things to remember who they were and what they stood for. They are called the five Ks because, in each case, the Panjabi name begins with the letter K.

The first is *Kes*, which means hair. He told them never to cut their hair. The uncut hair on the head or face shows a Sikh's *faith in God*.

The other four are things that Sikhs should wear:
Kangha is a small comb. It is usually made of wood, ivory or plastic. It shows the importance of *cleanliness* of the hair which has been made sacred by anointing it with amrit. Men tuck the kangha in the top knot of their hair and a turban is tied over it. Women also tuck a kangha in their hair.
Kara is a steel ring that looks like a bracelet and is worn on the right wrist. It shows the *unbreakable bond* of all Sikhs with their Guru and with each other. The kara is not worn as an ornament.
Kaccha, also called kashera, is a pair of knee-length shorts used as underwear. It shows *modesty* in all respects.
Kirpan is a sword. It gives confidence and shows self-respect but most importantly it represents justice and freedom.

All initiated Sikhs are expected to wear these symbols to show they belong to the Khalsa. In this way they remind themselves to be strong in body, mind and soul.

> The guiding principles of a Sikh's daily life can be stated like this:
> 1 **Nam Japo** – meaning to recite the name of God, which Sikhs do in five prayers, called banies. These are recited everyday at different times of the day.

2 **Kirt Karo** – meaning to earn an honest living. For this reason, amongst other things, Sikhs must not gamble.
3 **Wand Chako** – meaning to share your earnings with others; not only your own family but with others who are needy or poor.

● It is also true that most religious Sikhs are strict vegetarians. Why do you think this is so?

● Look back at your own rules or principles and the way you decided to remember them. Compare them to the five Ks of the Sikhs. Discuss the value of the five Ks as ways of remembering the principles they stand for.

Sikh names

Apart from their code of conduct, Sikhs also take pride in their names. A Sikh baby receives his or her name in the gurdwara. The first letter is chosen by opening the Guru Granth Sahib at random. The parents decide on the name which must begin with the first letter of the first word of the first verse on the left-hand page of the Guru Granth Sahib.

● How did your parents choose your name and what does it mean?

Can you identify the five Ks this man is wearing?

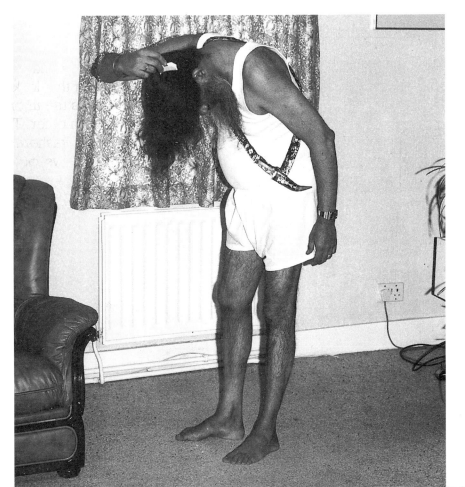

Key Words

Nam Japo   Kirt Karo
Wand Chako

21   The Sikh turban

The turban is a very important part of a Sikh man's clothing, which he treats like a crown. He remembers that his very first turban was tied ceremoniously, in front of the Guru Granth Sahib and the congregation. A Sikh thinks it an honour when he is presented with a turban as an award for outstanding service. Material for a turban, about five metres long and one metre wide, always makes an appropriate gift, whatever the occasion. Very close friends can exchange their turbans to act like blood brothers.

Satpal Singh Panesar is a 16-year-old boy. He remembers the day when his first turban was tied on his head:

Satpal Singh Panesar

"My first turban was tied when I was eight years old. The turban tying ceremony was performed at home. My parents bought a length of muslin material. My mother washed the material, dyed it light pink and lightly starched it. A starched turban keeps its shape better. My parents had also arranged for a kirtan one Sunday morning. So a copy of the Guru Granth Sahib was installed in our lounge which was cleared of all belongings. Family friends and relatives were invited to the ceremony. I had a bath in the morning, as this is essential for any religious ceremony. I got dressed in new clothes.

"When the kirtan was over, I was asked to sit in front of the Guru Granth Sahib. Everybody was looking at me. My parents had asked my uncle to tie the first turban on my head. I was nervous. My uncle placed the 'lar' (one end of the turban) in my left hand and wound the rest of the turban material round my head. The end of the material in my uncle's hand was tucked in the front of my turban and the end in my left hand was tucked at the back. When the turban had been tied it felt gentle and warm on my head. I felt more relaxed. I also felt like a proper Guru's Sikh. My parents felt proud of me. Everybody present congratulated my parents and myself. As this was a happy occasion I was given gifts, mainly token money in cash. The Granthi in his prayer for me wished me to preserve the turban on my head, for my hair and my turban are a symbol of my vow to live for the love of God and my Gurus. Everybody was served Karah Parshad and treated to a sumptuous lunch.

A giani tying a turban on a boy's head in the presence of his family and the congregation.

At school

"The next day I went to school. The non-Sikh kids teased me and even though I felt hurt, I ignored them. My best friend comforted me by saying that I looked better with a turban. When I returned home, everything looked as if it had changed for me. I felt as if I was a grown-up with big responsibilities. My younger brother treated me like a proper big brother. Some change must have come over me.

"My parents helped me with turban tying in the first few months and then I began to tie it myself. It takes only a few minutes to tie a turban. I can tie any style I want, though I like certain styles better than others.

"I am now 16 and of the things giani ji told me about the turban I remember one thing clearly. He said, 'Son, as a member of the Sikh community you must follow the ways of the Gurus, and to do this you must fully understand the meaning of Sabat Surat Dastar Sira.' This verse from the Sikh scriptures means that only with the turban on is your appearance complete."

● Do you have a special item of clothing you like to wear? It might be something you are really proud of, perhaps a coat, a hat, or a pair of shoes. Write down what it is and try to explain why you like to wear it. Share this with your class.

45

The Sikh calendar

Sikhs follow the Indian lunar calendar to work out the dates of festivals. Each lunar month is the time between two new moons. The lunar calendar is divided into 12 months and as the lunar year is shorter than the solar year, an extra month is added every third year. The first month is called "chaiter" in Panjabi. It falls somewhere between March and April. The Sikh New Year begins on the first day of Vaisakhi, the second month of the Indian lunar calendar. Except for the Vaisakhi festival which has a fixed date of 13 April (on rare occasions 14 April), the dates of all other festivals vary from one year to another.

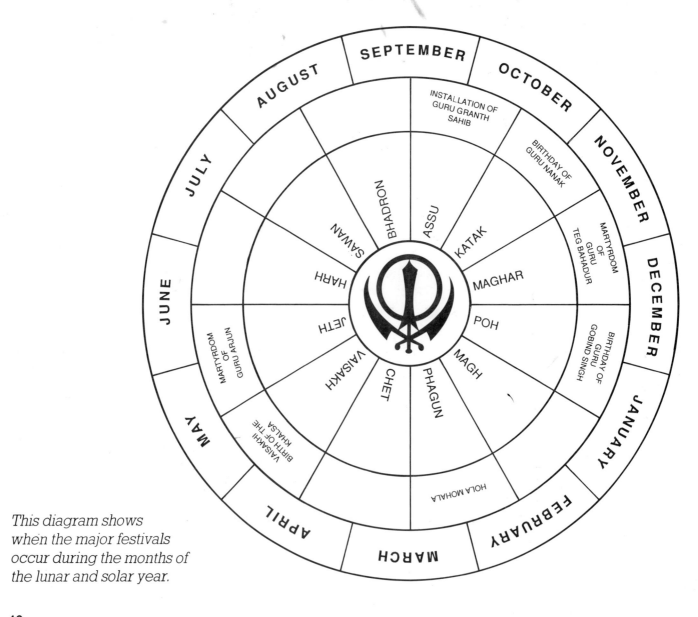

This diagram shows when the major festivals occur during the months of the lunar and solar year.

Glossary

Adi Granth	The Sikh holy book; came to be known as Guru Granth Sahib when Guru *Gobind Singh* installed it as his successor.
Akhand Path	Continuous reading of the Guru Granth Sahib completed in 48 hours.
amrit	Baptismal water; solution of water and sugar (patasa) prepared whilst reciting a set of five prayers and used at the initiation ceremony.
Ardas	Sikh prayer said at the end of a service; or at the beginning of an occasion as a prayer for its successful completion.
Arjun Dev	The fifth Guru of the Sikhs.
Amar Das	The third Guru of the Sikhs.
Asa di Var	Long hymn written by Guru Nanak in praise of God and in hope of finding Him; always sung in the early hours of the morning.
duppatta	Long scarf used by women and made of fine, lightweight materials.
Gobind Rai	Guru Gobind Singh's original name.
Gobind Singh	Gobind Rai's name after his own initiation by the *Panj Pyare*.
Golden Temple	The most sacred gurdwara of the Sikhs in the city of Amritsar in India.
Granth Sahib	The book of Sikh scriptures.
Granthi	Person who looks after the Guru Granth Sahib and is able to read it too.
Gurbani	Words of the Gurus as found in the Guru Granth Sahib.
gurdwara	Sikh place of worship.
gurpurbs	Sikh festivals mainly commemorating events in the lives of the Gurus.
Guru Ka Langar	Food cooked and served from a *gurdwara*'s community kitchen.
Hola Maholla	Sikh festival, full of activities such as mock fights, held on the day of Holi.
Hukumnamah	Random reading taken as a source of guidance from the Guru Granth Sahib.
Kabaddi	Traditional game played at the Sikh festival of *Hola Maholla*.
kirpan	Sword; one of the five Ks (see pages 42–43).
kirtan	Hymns played by ragis and sung by the congregation.
Kirt Karo	To earn an honest living.
Mool Mantar	Guru Nanak's description of God.
Nam Japo	To recite the name of God.
Nanak	The first Guru of the Sikhs.
Panj Pyare	The Beloved Five; the original Five who were initiated by Guru Gobind Singh.
pundits	Brahmin priests.
Punjab	The land of five rivers; a state in north-western India.
Ram Das	The fourth Guru of the Sikhs.
sangat	Congregation; assembly for worship.
sewa	Selfless service.
shabeel	Distribution of free soft drinks along the roads and streets during a procession especially at the time of Guru Arjun's *Shahidi* gurpurb.
Shahidi	Martyrdom.
sharbat	Popular drink made by mixing milk, cold water and sugar.
Teg Bahadur	The ninth Guru of the Sikhs.
turban	Headgear of a male Sikh; called Pug or Dastar in Punjabi.
Wand Chako	To share one's earnings (food) with others.

LONGMAN GROUP UK LIMITED,
Longman House, Burnt Mill, Harlow,
Essex CM20 2JE, England
and Associated Companies throughout the world.

First published 1989

Set in Linotron 202 on 12/14 point Rockwell Light
Produced by Longman Group (FE) Ltd
Printed in Hong Kong

ISBN 0 582 31787 8

We are grateful to the following for permission to reproduce photographs:

A.S. Choudry, page 20; O. Cole, page 6; E. Nesbitt, page 7 (below); H.S. Jabbal, pages
28, 45. Ann & Bury Peerless Slide Resources & Picture Library, cover and pages 7 (above), 34
Picturepoint Ltd, pages 5, 58; Daljeet Singh, page 18.
All other photographs were supplied by G.S. Babraa.